The Power of Connection: Exploring Relationship Patterns and Personality Development

Kevin

Copyright © [2023]

Title: The Power of Connection: Exploring Relationship Patterns and Personality Development
Author's: Kevin

All rights reserved. No part of this publication may be reproduced, stored in a retrieval system, or transmitted in any form or by any means, electronic, mechanical, photocopying, recording, or otherwise, without the prior written permission of the publisher or author, except in the case of brief quotations embodied in critical reviews and certain other non-commercial uses permitted by copyright law.

This book was printed and published by [Publisher's: **Kevin**] in [2023]

ISBN:

TABLE OF CONTENT

Chapter 1: Introduction   08

The importance of relationships in shaping personality development

Overview of relationship patterns and their impact on personality

Purpose and structure of the book

Chapter 2: Understanding Relationship Patterns   15

Definition and concept of relationship patterns

Factors influencing the formation of relationship patterns

Types of relationship patterns

The role of early childhood experiences in shaping relationship patterns

Chapter 3: The Link Between Relationship Patterns and Personality Development 23

How relationship patterns influence personality development

The impact of healthy relationship patterns on personality

The connection between relationship patterns and personality disorders

Identifying and understanding dysfunctional relationship patterns

Chapter 4: Exploring Personality Disorders 31

Overview of personality disorders

Common personality disorders associated with relationship patterns

Symptoms and characteristics of personality disorders

The interplay between relationship patterns and personality disorders

Chapter 5: Narcissistic Personality Disorder and Relationship Patterns — 39

Understanding narcissism and its impact on relationships

The development of narcissistic personality disorder

Relationship patterns commonly observed in individuals with narcissistic personality disorder

Strategies for dealing with narcissistic individuals

Chapter 6: Borderline Personality Disorder and Relationship Patterns — 47

An overview of borderline personality disorder

Relationship patterns often seen in individuals with borderline personality disorder

The impact of relationship patterns on the symptoms of borderline personality disorder

Approaches to managing relationships with individuals with borderline personality disorder

Chapter 7: Antisocial Personality Disorder and Relationship Patterns 55

Understanding antisocial personality disorder and its relationship patterns

The development of antisocial personality disorder

Relationship patterns commonly observed in individuals with antisocial personality disorder

Coping strategies for interacting with individuals with antisocial personality disorder

Chapter 8: Avoidant Personality Disorder and Relationship Patterns 63

An overview of avoidant personality disorder

Relationship patterns often seen in individuals with avoidant personality disorder

The impact of relationship patterns on the symptoms of avoidant personality disorder

Approaches to building healthy relationships with individuals with avoidant personality disorder

Chapter 9: Healing and Transforming Relationship Patterns — 71

Recognizing and acknowledging unhealthy relationship patterns

Strategies for breaking free from dysfunctional relationship patterns

Building healthy relationship patterns for personal growth and development

Seeking professional help for healing and transforming relationship patterns

Chapter 10: Conclusion — 79

Recap of key points discussed in the book

The importance of self-awareness and self-reflection in relationship patterns

Embracing healthy relationship patterns for personal and interpersonal growth

Final thoughts on the power of connection and its impact on personality development

Chapter 1: Introduction

The importance of relationships in shaping personality development

Relationships play a profound role in shaping our personality and influencing our overall development. From the moment we are born, our interactions with others begin to mold our thoughts, emotions, and behaviors. In the book "The Power of Connection: Exploring Relationship Patterns and Personality Development," we delve into the crucial role that relationships play in the formation of our personalities, and how they can impact the development and manifestation of personality disorders.

Every one of us is born with a unique set of traits and tendencies, but it is through our relationships with parents, siblings, friends, and even strangers that these qualities are nurtured and developed. The quality of these early relationships is particularly significant, as they lay the foundation for our emotional well-being and social skills. Warm, supportive relationships foster a sense of security and allow us to explore the world confidently, while relationships characterized by neglect, abuse, or inconsistency can hinder our growth and contribute to the development of personality disorders.

Personality disorders are deeply ingrained patterns of behavior and thought that deviate significantly from the societal norm. They often manifest in repetitive and maladaptive ways of relating to oneself and others, causing distress and impairment in various areas of life. While genetic factors and individual temperament certainly play a role in the development of personality disorders, it is the quality of our relationships that can greatly influence whether these tendencies are exacerbated or mitigated.

Children who grow up in environments characterized by instability, trauma, or emotional neglect are at a higher risk of developing personality disorders later in life. For example, a child who experiences physical abuse may develop a pattern of aggressive behavior as a means of self-protection. Similarly, a child who is constantly criticized or invalidated may struggle with low self-esteem and develop avoidant or dependent personality traits.

On the other hand, healthy, nurturing relationships can serve as protective factors, buffering individuals from the development of personality disorders. A child who grows up in a secure and loving environment is more likely to develop a positive sense of self and healthy coping mechanisms. Positive relationships provide emotional support, teach problem-solving skills, and promote self-reflection, all of which contribute to a healthier personality development.

Understanding the importance of relationships in shaping personality development is not only relevant for individuals experiencing personality disorders but for every one of us. By recognizing the impact that our interactions have on others, we can strive to build and maintain healthy relationships, fostering positive growth and development for ourselves and those around us.

Overview of relationship patterns and their impact on personality

Introduction:

Understanding the intricate relationship between our patterns of relating to others and the development of our personality is crucial for personal growth and healthy interpersonal connections. In this subchapter, we will delve into the causes of personality disorders and explore how different relationship patterns can shape our personalities. By recognizing the impact of these patterns, we can gain valuable insights into our own behavior and make positive changes for a more fulfilling life.

The Causes of Personality Disorders:

Personality disorders are characterized by deeply ingrained patterns of behavior, thoughts, and emotions that deviate from societal norms. While the causes of personality disorders are multifaceted, it is widely believed that they stem from a combination of genetic, environmental, and relational factors. In particular, the nature of one's relationships during childhood and adolescence can significantly influence the development of personality disorders.

Patterns of Relating and Personality Development:

Our relationships serve as a mirror, reflecting back to us how we perceive ourselves and others. The patterns we establish in our relationships, whether healthy or dysfunctional, can have a profound impact on our personality development. For example, individuals who consistently experience rejection or abandonment may develop a fear of intimacy, leading to avoidant or borderline personality traits.

Furthermore, the way we interact with others shapes our self-image and self-esteem. If we consistently find ourselves in toxic relationships characterized by manipulation or control, we may develop narcissistic or dependent personality traits. Conversely, healthy relationships built on trust, respect, and open communication can foster positive personality traits such as empathy, resilience, and self-confidence.

Recognizing and Changing Patterns:

Awareness is the first step towards breaking free from destructive relationship patterns and healing our personalities. By reflecting on past experiences and examining our current relationships, we can identify recurring themes and behaviors that may be holding us back. It is essential to seek professional help if necessary, as therapists can provide valuable guidance and support throughout the process.

Changing deeply ingrained patterns requires dedication and perseverance. It involves learning new ways of relating to others, developing healthy boundaries, and challenging negative beliefs about ourselves. Through consistent effort and a willingness to grow, we can transform our relationship patterns and cultivate a healthier, more authentic version of ourselves.

Conclusion:

Our relationships have a profound impact on our personality development. By understanding the causes of personality disorders and recognizing the influence of our relationship patterns, we can take control of our lives and create healthier, more fulfilling connections. Remember, change is possible, and with the right support and effort, we can break free from destructive patterns and cultivate a more positive and authentic self.

Purpose and structure of the book

In "The Power of Connection: Exploring Relationship Patterns and Personality Development," we delve into the intricate and fascinating world of personality disorders. This subchapter aims to provide a comprehensive understanding of the purpose and structure of the book, as well as the causes of personality disorders, making it accessible and relevant to everyone.

The purpose of this book is to shed light on the complex web of relationship patterns and their impact on personality development. Whether you are a professional in the field of psychology or simply someone seeking to better understand yourself and the people around you, this book offers valuable insights into the causes and dynamics of personality disorders.

The book is divided into various sections, each focusing on specific aspects related to personality disorders. The structure is designed to provide a systematic approach to understanding these disorders, starting with an introduction to personality development and the role of relationships in shaping our personalities. By examining the influence of early childhood experiences, familial dynamics, and societal factors, we aim to unravel the intricate tapestry of personality development.

Furthermore, the book delves into the various types of personality disorders, exploring their unique characteristics and diagnostic criteria. From narcissistic and borderline personality disorders to antisocial and avoidant personality disorders, we aim to illuminate the intricacies of each condition. Through case studies and real-life examples, we provide a relatable and comprehensive understanding of these disorders, allowing readers to identify and empathize with individuals who may be experiencing them.

Moreover, this book also aims to address the underlying causes of personality disorders. By exploring the interplay between genetics, neurobiology, and environmental factors, we provide a holistic understanding of why these disorders arise. The book aims to dispel common misconceptions and stigmas surrounding personality disorders, fostering empathy and compassion towards those who may be suffering from them.

In conclusion, "The Power of Connection: Exploring Relationship Patterns and Personality Development" is a comprehensive guide that aims to demystify personality disorders. Whether you are a professional seeking to expand your knowledge or an individual looking to understand yourself and others better, this book provides valuable insights into the causes and dynamics of these disorders. By delving into the purpose and structure of the book, we invite every reader to embark on a transformative journey of understanding and compassion.

Chapter 2: Understanding Relationship Patterns

Definition and concept of relationship patterns

Relationship patterns play a vital role in our lives and have a significant impact on our personality development. Understanding these patterns is essential for maintaining healthy relationships and preventing the development of personality disorders. In this subchapter, we will delve into the definition and concept of relationship patterns and explore their connection to personality development.

Relationship patterns refer to the recurring ways in which individuals interact with others in their personal and professional lives. These patterns are shaped by our upbringing, past experiences, and the beliefs and values we hold. They influence the way we communicate, handle conflicts, and form emotional bonds with others. Relationship patterns can be both positive and negative, and they have a profound influence on our overall well-being.

It is important to recognize that relationship patterns are not fixed or unchangeable. They are malleable and can be modified with self-awareness, introspection, and personal growth. By understanding our relationship patterns, we can gain insights into our behaviors, motivations, and the impact we have on others.

In the context of personality development, relationship patterns are closely linked to the causes of personality disorders. Personality disorders are characterized by long-term patterns of thoughts, feelings, and behaviors that deviate from societal norms. They often result in difficulties in forming and maintaining healthy relationships.

Certain relationship patterns, such as a pattern of emotional detachment or a pattern of aggressive behavior, can contribute to the development of personality disorders. For example, individuals who have experienced a lack of emotional support or have been subjected to abuse during childhood may develop patterns of mistrust, avoidance, or aggression in their relationships.

By exploring relationship patterns, we can gain a deeper understanding of the causes of personality disorders. This knowledge empowers us to recognize and address unhealthy patterns in ourselves and in others, promoting healthier relationships and overall well-being.

In conclusion, relationship patterns are the recurring ways in which individuals interact with others. They significantly impact our personality development and can contribute to the causes of personality disorders. By understanding and modifying our relationship patterns, we can foster healthier relationships and prevent the development of personality disorders. This knowledge is valuable for everyone, regardless of their background or interests, as it enables us to cultivate meaningful connections and lead more fulfilling lives.

Factors influencing the formation of relationship patterns

In order to understand the causes of personality disorders and the subsequent impact on relationship patterns, it is crucial to explore the various factors that contribute to their formation. This subchapter aims to shed light on these influential factors and their role in shaping our connections with others.

1. Childhood experiences: Our early experiences play a significant role in shaping our relationship patterns. Traumatic events, neglect, abuse, or inconsistent parental care can lead to the development of maladaptive coping mechanisms and difficulties in forming healthy relationships later in life.

2. Attachment styles: Attachment theory suggests that our early attachment experiences with primary caregivers shape our expectations and behaviors in relationships. Secure attachment fosters healthy relationship patterns, while insecure attachment styles, such as avoidant or anxious attachment, can lead to difficulties in forming and maintaining connections.

3. Family dynamics: The family environment and dynamics significantly influence the formation of relationship patterns. Dysfunctional family systems, characterized by conflict, poor communication, or emotional neglect, can contribute to the development of personality disorders and maladaptive relationship patterns.

4. Genetics and biology: Research suggests that genetics and biological factors contribute to the susceptibility of personality disorders. Certain genetic predispositions, combined with environmental factors, can

increase the likelihood of developing specific disorders that influence relationship patterns.

5. Cultural and societal influences: Cultural and societal norms, values, and expectations shape our understanding of relationships. Societal factors such as gender roles, cultural traditions, and societal pressures can influence the formation of relationship patterns and contribute to the development of personality disorders.

6. Trauma and life events: Traumatic experiences, such as physical or emotional abuse, loss, or significant life events, can have a profound impact on our relationship patterns. Trauma can result in difficulties with trust, emotional regulation, and interpersonal boundaries, affecting the quality of our connections.

7. Personal beliefs and self-perception: Our personal beliefs, self-perception, and self-esteem influence the formation of relationship patterns. Negative self-perception or distorted beliefs about oneself can lead to difficulties in establishing and maintaining healthy relationships.

Understanding the factors that influence the formation of relationship patterns is essential for recognizing the causes of personality disorders and their impact on our connections with others. By gaining insight into these factors, individuals can work towards personal growth, healing, and the development of healthier relationship patterns. Whether you are personally affected by these issues or are interested in understanding them for a loved one, this subchapter will provide valuable insights into the complexities of relationship patterns and personality development.

Types of relationship patterns

In order to understand the causes of personality disorders, it is crucial to explore the various types of relationship patterns that individuals may exhibit. Relationship patterns are a fundamental aspect of personality development and can greatly influence our interactions with others. By examining these patterns, we can gain insight into the underlying factors that contribute to the development of personality disorders.

1. Codependent Relationships: Codependency is a common relationship pattern characterized by excessive reliance on others for self-esteem and identity. Individuals in codependent relationships often prioritize the needs of their partner over their own, leading to a loss of personal autonomy. This pattern can contribute to the development of personality disorders such as dependent personality disorder.

2. Avoidant Relationships: Some individuals tend to avoid intimacy and closeness in relationships due to fear of rejection or abandonment. Avoidant relationship patterns are marked by emotional distance and a reluctance to engage in deep emotional connections. These patterns can contribute to the development of avoidant personality disorder.

3. Narcissistic Relationships: Narcissistic relationship patterns involve a disproportionate focus on oneself and a lack of empathy towards others. Individuals with narcissistic tendencies may exploit and manipulate others to fulfill their own needs, leading to difficulties in maintaining healthy relationships. Narcissistic relationship patterns can contribute to the development of narcissistic personality disorder.

4. Borderline Relationships: Borderline relationship patterns are characterized by intense emotional instability, fear of abandonment, and a tendency towards impulsive behavior. Individuals with borderline personality disorder often struggle with maintaining stable and healthy relationships due to their extreme emotional fluctuations. These patterns can contribute to the development of borderline personality disorder.

5. Enmeshed Relationships: Enmeshed relationship patterns involve an excessive level of emotional fusion and blurred boundaries between individuals. In these relationships, personal identities become intertwined, leading to a lack of autonomy and individual growth. Enmeshed relationship patterns can contribute to the development of dependent personality disorder.

Understanding the various types of relationship patterns is crucial for identifying the causes of personality disorders. These patterns can shed light on the underlying dynamics that contribute to the development of maladaptive behaviors and dysfunctional relationships. By recognizing and addressing these patterns, individuals can work towards healthier and more fulfilling relationships, ultimately promoting their own personal growth and well-being.

The role of early childhood experiences in shaping relationship patterns

In the realm of psychology and human development, it is widely recognized that early childhood experiences play a pivotal role in shaping an individual's personality and their subsequent relationship patterns. Our formative years are a crucial time for learning and adaptation, and the experiences we have during this period can significantly influence our future relationships.

From the moment we are born, we begin to form attachments with our caregivers. These early relationships serve as the foundation for all future relationships we will have. If we are fortunate enough to have secure and nurturing attachments, we are more likely to develop healthy relationship patterns later in life. However, if our early experiences are characterized by neglect, abuse, or instability, it can have long-lasting effects on our ability to form and maintain healthy relationships.

Research has shown that individuals who have experienced trauma or adverse childhood experiences (ACEs) are at a higher risk of developing personality disorders. ACEs include physical, emotional, or sexual abuse, neglect, witnessing domestic violence, or growing up in a household with substance abuse or mental illness. These experiences can disrupt the normal development of a child's brain, leading to an increased vulnerability to developing maladaptive relationship patterns.

Children who grow up in chaotic or abusive environments may struggle with trust, emotional regulation, and forming secure attachments. They may develop anxious or avoidant attachment styles, making it difficult for them to establish healthy, intimate relationships in adulthood. Additionally, they may have difficulty setting boundaries, expressing emotions, and dealing with conflict, which can further contribute to the development of personality disorders.

Understanding the role of early childhood experiences in shaping relationship patterns is essential for the prevention and treatment of personality disorders. By providing support and interventions early on, we can help children develop healthier relationship patterns and reduce the risk of future psychological difficulties. This requires a multidisciplinary approach involving psychologists, educators, parents, and caregivers to create safe and nurturing environments that foster resilience and promote healthy relationship development.

In conclusion, early childhood experiences have a profound impact on an individual's relationship patterns and can contribute to the development of personality disorders. By recognizing the significance of these experiences and providing appropriate support and interventions, we can help individuals overcome the challenges they may face and cultivate healthy and fulfilling relationships.

Chapter 3: The Link Between Relationship Patterns and Personality Development

How relationship patterns influence personality development

In the journey of understanding ourselves and the intricacies of human behavior, it becomes crucial to explore how relationship patterns shape our personality development. This subchapter titled "How Relationship Patterns Influence Personality Development" delves deep into the powerful connection between our relationships and the formation of our personalities.

Personality disorders, often misunderstood and stigmatized, have complex causes. As we unravel the mysteries behind these disorders, it becomes evident that relationship patterns play a significant role in their development. This subchapter aims to shed light on this crucial aspect, offering valuable insights for EVERYONE interested in understanding the causes of personality disorders.

From early childhood, our personalities begin to take shape through interactions with our caregivers, family members, and close friends. These relationships form the foundation upon which our personalities develop. Positive, nurturing relationships foster healthy personality development, while negative or abusive relationships can lead to the manifestation of personality disorders.

By examining various relationship patterns, we can identify the factors that contribute to the development of personality disorders. For instance, individuals who have experienced consistent rejection or neglect during their formative years may develop avoidant or dependent personality disorders. On the other hand, those subjected to emotional or physical abuse may exhibit traits associated with borderline or antisocial personality disorders.

Understanding the impact of relationship patterns on personality development empowers us to recognize and address these issues effectively. By recognizing patterns of abuse, neglect, or unhealthy attachment, we can intervene early on, potentially preventing the onset or worsening of personality disorders. Additionally, gaining insight into how our own relationship patterns influence our personalities allows us to take responsibility for our actions and make positive changes in our lives.

By exploring the connection between relationship patterns and personality development, this subchapter aims to foster empathy, compassion, and understanding among EVERYONE. It provides a platform to discuss the causes of personality disorders openly, breaking down the stigma associated with these conditions.

The Power of Connection: Exploring Relationship Patterns and Personality Development is not just a book for specialists but for EVERYONE seeking a deep understanding of human behavior. By examining the causes of personality disorders through the lens of relationship patterns, this subchapter offers invaluable insights into the complexities of our personalities and the potential for growth and healing.

The impact of healthy relationship patterns on personality

In the journey of self-discovery and personal growth, it becomes crucial to explore the impact of healthy relationship patterns on the development of our personality. Relationships, whether with family, friends, or romantic partners, play a significant role in shaping who we are as individuals. This subchapter delves into the profound influence of healthy relationships on our personality development.

When we talk about healthy relationship patterns, we refer to those that are built on trust, respect, effective communication, and emotional support. These relationships provide a safe and nurturing environment for personal growth and self-expression. They foster a sense of belonging and encourage individuals to explore their true potential.

One cannot underestimate the transformative power of healthy relationships on our personality. They act as mirrors, reflecting back our strengths, weaknesses, and areas for improvement. Through these relationships, we gain invaluable insights into our own behavior, beliefs, and emotions. They offer a platform for self-reflection, introspection, and self-awareness, which are vital components of personality development.

Healthy relationships provide a solid foundation for emotional well-being. They offer a sense of security, emotional stability, and a support system during challenging times. When we feel valued and loved in our relationships, we develop a positive self-image, leading to enhanced self-esteem and confidence. This, in turn, shapes our personality, making us more resilient, adaptable, and open to new experiences.

Furthermore, healthy relationship patterns encourage personal growth and self-actualization. They provide opportunities for learning, self-discovery, and acquiring new skills. Through interactions with others, we gain different perspectives, broaden our horizons, and challenge our existing beliefs. This continuous process of growth and self-improvement contributes to the development of a well-rounded and mature personality.

On the other hand, the absence of healthy relationship patterns can have detrimental effects on personality development, leading to the emergence of personality disorders. When individuals grow up in dysfunctional or abusive relationships, they may develop maladaptive patterns of behavior, distorted self-perceptions, and difficulty in forming healthy relationships later in life. Understanding the causes and consequences of personality disorders is essential for individuals and professionals alike to address these issues effectively.

In conclusion, healthy relationship patterns have a profound impact on personality development. They offer a nurturing environment for self-discovery, emotional well-being, and personal growth. By fostering self-awareness, emotional stability, and resilience, healthy relationships contribute to the formation of a well-rounded and confident personality. Conversely, the absence of healthy relationship patterns can lead to the development of personality disorders. It is crucial for individuals to recognize the importance of cultivating healthy relationships and seek support when needed to ensure their own personal growth and well-being.

The connection between relationship patterns and personality disorders

In order to delve into the intricate world of personality disorders, it becomes imperative to understand the connection between relationship patterns and the development of these disorders. This subchapter aims to shed light on this critical link, exploring the causes of personality disorders and their relationship with our patterns of relating to others.

Personality disorders are complex mental health conditions that affect the way individuals think, feel, and behave. These disorders can have a profound impact on a person's ability to maintain healthy relationships and navigate social interactions. While the causes of personality disorders are multifaceted, research has shown that there is a strong correlation between early relationship patterns and the development of these disorders.

During childhood and adolescence, individuals develop their sense of self and learn how to relate to others primarily through their interactions with caregivers and significant others. These early relationships serve as the foundation for future social interactions, shaping our emotional well-being and influencing our personality development.

Children who experience neglect, abuse, or inconsistent care during their formative years are more likely to develop personality disorders later in life. These adverse experiences can disrupt healthy attachment patterns and lead to difficulties in forming and maintaining healthy relationships. For example, individuals who have experienced neglect may struggle with trust issues and have a heightened fear of rejection, while those who have been abused may exhibit aggressive or impulsive behaviors.

Furthermore, individuals with personality disorders often exhibit maladaptive relationship patterns characterized by intense emotions, unstable interpersonal connections, and a distorted sense of self. These patterns can perpetuate the development and maintenance of personality disorders, creating a vicious cycle that is difficult to break without intervention.

Understanding the connection between relationship patterns and personality disorders is essential for effective diagnosis, treatment, and prevention. By recognizing the impact of early relationships on personality development, mental health professionals can develop targeted interventions to address the underlying causes of these disorders. Additionally, individuals can gain insight into their own patterns of relating and take proactive steps towards healing and developing healthier relationships.

In conclusion, the connection between relationship patterns and personality disorders is a crucial aspect of understanding the causes and development of these complex mental health conditions. By exploring this connection, we can strive to create a society that fosters healthy relationships and supports individuals in their journey towards mental well-being. Whether you are a mental health professional, someone affected by personality disorders, or simply interested in the human mind, delving into this connection can provide valuable insights and contribute to a more compassionate and informed society.

Identifying and understanding dysfunctional relationship patterns

In the vast tapestry of human connections, relationships play a pivotal role in shaping our lives. They have the power to either empower or hinder our personal growth and development. However, not all relationships are healthy and nurturing. Some relationships can be marked by dysfunctional patterns that can have a profound impact on our mental and emotional well-being. In this subchapter, we delve into the realm of identifying and understanding these dysfunctional relationship patterns.

The causes of personality disorders

Personality disorders are complex mental health conditions that are characterized by deeply ingrained patterns of behavior, thinking, and feeling. They can significantly impair an individual's ability to function in various areas of life, including relationships. Understanding the causes of personality disorders is essential in identifying and addressing dysfunctional relationship patterns.

One of the primary causes of personality disorders is believed to be a combination of genetic and environmental factors. Genetic predispositions, such as certain temperaments or personality traits, can increase the likelihood of developing a personality disorder. However, it is important to note that genetics alone do not determine the outcome. Environmental factors, such as childhood experiences, trauma, neglect, or dysfunctional family dynamics, play a crucial role in the development of these disorders.

Dysfunctional relationship patterns often emerge as a result of these underlying causes. Individuals with personality disorders may struggle with interpersonal skills, have difficulty regulating their emotions, or exhibit destructive behaviors. These patterns can manifest in a variety of ways, such as codependency, emotional manipulation, frequent conflicts, or a lack of boundaries.

Identifying these dysfunctional relationship patterns is the first step towards healing and personal growth. It requires self-reflection, self-awareness, and a willingness to confront and address unhealthy dynamics. By recognizing these patterns, individuals can break free from the cycle of dysfunction and create healthier, more fulfilling relationships.

Furthermore, understanding dysfunctional relationship patterns can also help loved ones and support networks provide the necessary support and encouragement. By being aware of the causes and effects of personality disorders, friends, family members, and mental health professionals can offer empathy, understanding, and guidance to those struggling with these challenges.

In conclusion, identifying and understanding dysfunctional relationship patterns is crucial for personal growth and well-being. By exploring the causes of personality disorders and their impact on relationships, individuals can break free from unhealthy patterns and cultivate healthier connections. Whether you are personally affected by these issues or supporting someone who is, this subchapter provides valuable insights to navigate the complexities of dysfunctional relationships and foster positive change.

Chapter 4: Exploring Personality Disorders

Overview of personality disorders

Personality disorders are a complex and often misunderstood category of mental health conditions that affect a significant portion of the population. In this subchapter, we will delve into the causes of personality disorders, exploring the intricate interplay between genetic, environmental, and social factors that contribute to their development.

Understanding personality disorders requires a comprehensive examination of various dimensions. These disorders encompass a range of behavioral, emotional, and cognitive patterns that deviate significantly from societal norms and cause impairment in daily functioning. They can manifest in various ways, including difficulties in forming and maintaining relationships, impulsivity, emotional instability, and distorted self-perception.

Research suggests that personality disorders are influenced by a combination of genetic predisposition and environmental factors. Studies have shown that certain personality traits have a hereditary component, meaning that individuals may be genetically more prone to developing specific disorders. However, it is important to note that genetics alone do not determine the presence of a personality disorder, and environmental factors play a crucial role in their manifestation.

Childhood experiences and upbringing also significantly impact the development of personality disorders. Adverse childhood events such as neglect, abuse, or inconsistent parenting can contribute to the formation of maladaptive patterns of thinking and behavior. These early experiences shape an individual's worldview, self-perception, and ability to regulate emotions, all of which are essential components of personality development.

Moreover, societal and cultural factors can influence the prevalence and expression of personality disorders. Societal expectations, cultural norms, and social pressures can contribute to the development of specific personality traits or patterns that may be considered disordered. For example, in certain cultures, traits such as emotional expressiveness or assertiveness may be stigmatized, leading individuals to suppress these aspects of their personality, potentially resulting in disorders such as Avoidant or Dependent Personality Disorder.

It is crucial to approach the topic of personality disorders with empathy and understanding. It is not uncommon for individuals with personality disorders to face stigma and discrimination, further exacerbating their struggles. By gaining a deeper understanding of the causes and complexities of these disorders, we can foster a more compassionate and supportive society.

In the subsequent chapters of this book, we will delve into specific types of personality disorders, exploring their unique characteristics, diagnostic criteria, and treatment approaches. By examining these disorders through a lens of connection and relationship patterns, we aim to provide insights that can help individuals navigate their interpersonal relationships more effectively, both personally and professionally.

Common personality disorders associated with relationship patterns

Common personality disorders associated with relationship patterns can greatly impact our lives and the way we interact with others. These disorders can make it difficult to maintain healthy and fulfilling relationships, causing strain and distress for both individuals involved. In this subchapter, we will explore some of the most common personality disorders that are often associated with relationship patterns.

One such disorder is borderline personality disorder (BPD). People with BPD often struggle with instability in their relationships, intense fear of abandonment, and emotional dysregulation. They may exhibit impulsive behaviors, have difficulty trusting others, and experience intense and rapidly shifting emotions. These characteristics can create a volatile and unpredictable dynamic within relationships, making it challenging for individuals with BPD to form lasting and secure connections.

Another commonly observed personality disorder is narcissistic personality disorder (NPD). Individuals with NPD often display an exaggerated sense of self-importance, a need for excessive admiration, and a lack of empathy for others. These traits can lead to difficulties in maintaining healthy relationships, as individuals with NPD may prioritize their own needs and desires above those of their partners. They may also struggle with taking responsibility for their actions and may exhibit manipulative behaviors to maintain control within the relationship.

Antisocial personality disorder (ASPD) is yet another personality disorder that can significantly impact relationship patterns. Individuals with ASPD often display a disregard for the rights of others, a lack of remorse or empathy, and a tendency towards impulsive and aggressive behaviors. These characteristics can make it challenging for individuals with ASPD to form and maintain meaningful relationships, as their actions may harm others or lead to a lack of trust and emotional intimacy.

While the causes of personality disorders are often complex and multifaceted, they can be influenced by a combination of genetic, environmental, and psychological factors. Childhood trauma, such as abuse or neglect, can contribute to the development of personality disorders. Additionally, certain genetic predispositions and brain abnormalities may also play a role.

Understanding these common personality disorders and their associated relationship patterns can provide valuable insights into our own behaviors and the behaviors of those around us. By recognizing the signs and symptoms, we can seek appropriate support and treatment to foster healthier and more fulfilling relationships. Developing empathy, communication skills, and setting healthy boundaries can also be beneficial in navigating relationships with individuals who may have these personality disorders. Ultimately, building awareness and understanding can empower us to create more positive and compassionate connections with others.

Symptoms and characteristics of personality disorders

Personality disorders are complex mental health conditions that can significantly impact an individual's thoughts, emotions, and behaviors. Understanding the symptoms and characteristics of these disorders is crucial in order to recognize and seek appropriate help for those affected. In this subchapter, we will delve into the intricacies of personality disorders and shed light on their diverse manifestations.

One crucial aspect of personality disorders is the presence of persistent and rigid patterns of thinking, feeling, and behaving that deviate from societal norms. These patterns, ingrained over time, can cause significant distress and impairment in various areas of life, such as relationships, work, and overall functioning.

There are several types of personality disorders, each with its own unique set of symptoms and characteristics. For example, individuals with borderline personality disorder may experience intense and unstable relationships, impulsivity, emotional instability, and a distorted sense of self. On the other hand, those with narcissistic personality disorder may exhibit grandiosity, a constant need for admiration, a lack of empathy, and an exaggerated sense of entitlement.

Other common types of personality disorders include avoidant personality disorder, which is characterized by extreme social inhibition, feelings of inadequacy, and a strong fear of rejection. Antisocial personality disorder involves a disregard for others' rights, a lack of remorse, and a tendency towards manipulative and exploitative behaviors. Obsessive-compulsive personality disorder is marked by perfectionism, rigid adherence to rules, and an excessive need for control.

It is important to note that individuals with personality disorders may not necessarily exhibit all the symptoms associated with a specific disorder. Additionally, symptoms can vary in intensity and may be triggered by certain situations or stressors.

Understanding the causes of personality disorders is a complex and ongoing area of research. While there is no single cause, a combination of genetic, environmental, and developmental factors can contribute to their development. For instance, childhood trauma, abuse, neglect, or inconsistent parenting can increase the risk of developing a personality disorder.

Recognizing the symptoms and characteristics of personality disorders is crucial in order to provide appropriate support and treatment. It is important to approach these individuals with empathy, understanding, and non-judgmental attitudes. Seeking professional help from mental health practitioners, such as psychologists or psychiatrists, is essential for diagnosis, treatment planning, and managing these disorders effectively.

In conclusion, personality disorders are complex mental health conditions that can significantly impact an individual's life. By understanding their symptoms and characteristics, we can foster empathy and create a supportive environment for those affected. Furthermore, recognizing the causes of personality disorders can aid in prevention and early intervention strategies, promoting healthier and more fulfilling lives for individuals and their loved ones.

The interplay between relationship patterns and personality disorders

The interplay between relationship patterns and personality disorders is a fascinating topic that sheds light on the complex nature of human behavior and development. In order to understand the causes of personality disorders, it is essential to explore the intricate relationship between our interpersonal dynamics and the development of these disorders.

Personality disorders are characterized by enduring patterns of thoughts, feelings, and behaviors that deviate from societal expectations. They often result in significant distress and impairment in various areas of life. While the causes of personality disorders are multifaceted, research has consistently shown that relationship patterns play a crucial role in their development.

Our early relationships, particularly with primary caregivers, shape the foundation of our personality. The quality of these relationships greatly influences our sense of self, our emotional regulation abilities, and our capacity for healthy connections with others. When these relationships are marked by neglect, abuse, or inconsistent care, it can lead to the development of personality disorders later in life.

For example, individuals who grow up in environments where they constantly face criticism, rejection, or emotional invalidation may develop traits associated with borderline personality disorder. The lack of consistent emotional support and validation can lead to intense fear of abandonment, unstable self-image, and difficulty regulating emotions. Similarly, individuals who experience chronic neglect or abuse may develop traits associated with antisocial or narcissistic personality disorders, as they learn to manipulate and exploit others to meet their needs.

Furthermore, the interplay between relationship patterns and personality disorders is not limited to childhood experiences. In adulthood, individuals with personality disorders often struggle to maintain healthy relationships due to their maladaptive patterns of thinking and behavior. Their difficulties in forming and maintaining stable connections can further perpetuate their symptoms and exacerbate their existing condition.

Understanding the interplay between relationship patterns and personality disorders is crucial for effective treatment and intervention strategies. By addressing the underlying relationship dynamics, therapists and individuals can work towards healing and developing healthier patterns of interaction. Additionally, raising awareness about the causes of personality disorders can help society to become more compassionate and supportive towards individuals who struggle with these conditions.

In conclusion, the interplay between relationship patterns and personality disorders is a complex and multifaceted topic. By exploring the causes of personality disorders, particularly the impact of early relationship experiences, we can gain insight into the development and maintenance of these conditions. This knowledge can facilitate more effective interventions and support for individuals with personality disorders, ultimately leading to improved mental health and well-being for all.

Chapter 5: Narcissistic Personality Disorder and Relationship Patterns

Understanding narcissism and its impact on relationships

Narcissism is a personality disorder that affects individuals in various aspects of their lives, especially in the realm of personal relationships. In this subchapter, we will explore the concept of narcissism and delve into its impact on relationships, shedding light on the causes of personality disorders.

Narcissism is characterized by an excessive preoccupation with oneself, a lack of empathy for others, and an inflated sense of self-importance. Those who exhibit narcissistic traits often have an intense need for admiration and validation from others. They manipulate and exploit others to fulfill their own desires, often disregarding the feelings and needs of those around them.

In relationships, narcissism can be highly detrimental. Narcissistic individuals often struggle with forming deep, meaningful connections with others. They prioritize their own needs and desires above all else, making it challenging for them to truly empathize with their partners. As a result, their relationships tend to be one-sided, with the narcissist demanding constant attention and admiration, while neglecting the emotional needs of their partner.

The impact of narcissism on relationships can be profound. Partners of narcissists often find themselves feeling unimportant, unseen, and emotionally drained. They may constantly try to please the narcissist, hoping to earn their love and validation, but find themselves in an endless cycle of disappointment and frustration. The lack of empathy and emotional support from the narcissist can lead to feelings of loneliness and even depression in the partner.

Understanding the causes of personality disorders, including narcissism, is crucial in addressing these issues. While the exact causes of narcissism are complex and multifaceted, research suggests that a combination of genetic, environmental, and psychological factors contribute to its development. Childhood experiences, such as neglect, abuse, or excessive praise, can shape the development of narcissistic traits.

By recognizing and understanding narcissism and its impact on relationships, individuals can better navigate their own relationships and support loved ones who may be affected by narcissistic personality disorder. Developing healthy boundaries, fostering open communication, and seeking professional help can all be effective strategies in dealing with narcissistic tendencies in relationships.

In conclusion, narcissism can have a significant impact on personal relationships. Understanding the causes of personality disorders, including narcissism, is essential in addressing these issues and fostering healthier connections. By educating ourselves about narcissism and its effects, we can create a more compassionate and empathetic society where relationships thrive.

The development of narcissistic personality disorder

The development of narcissistic personality disorder is a complex process that involves various factors and influences. Understanding how this disorder develops is crucial in order to effectively address and treat it. In this subchapter, we will delve into the intricate journey of narcissistic personality disorder development, shedding light on its causes and contributing factors.

Narcissistic personality disorder (NPD) typically emerges during adolescence or early adulthood, although some traits may be evident during childhood. It is characterized by an inflated sense of self-importance, a constant need for admiration and attention, and a lack of empathy towards others. It is important to note that not all individuals with narcissistic traits develop a full-blown disorder, as it depends on a combination of genetic, environmental, and psychological factors.

Genetic predisposition plays a significant role in the development of personality disorders, including NPD. Research suggests that certain genetic variations may make individuals more susceptible to developing narcissistic traits. However, it is important to remember that genetics alone do not determine the development of NPD; rather, they interact with environmental factors to shape one's personality.

Childhood experiences also contribute to the development of narcissistic personality disorder. Individuals who have experienced excessive praise or neglect during their formative years may develop an inflated sense of self-worth or an insatiable need for validation. On the other hand, those who have been subjected to abuse, criticism, or neglect may develop narcissistic traits as a defense mechanism to protect their fragile self-esteem.

Furthermore, societal and cultural influences play a crucial role in the development of NPD. In a society that glorifies individual success, power, and material possessions, individuals may be driven to adopt narcissistic behaviors in order to meet societal expectations and gain social acceptance. The rise of social media and the constant need for validation and attention have also contributed to the increase in narcissistic traits among individuals.

In conclusion, the development of narcissistic personality disorder is a multifaceted process that involves a combination of genetic predisposition, childhood experiences, and societal influences. Understanding these factors is essential in order to identify and address the root causes of NPD. By comprehending the complex nature of this disorder, we can work towards developing effective interventions and treatments that promote healthier relationship patterns and personality development.

Relationship patterns commonly observed in individuals with narcissistic personality disorder

Narcissistic personality disorder (NPD) is a complex and often misunderstood mental health condition. Characterized by an inflated sense of self-importance, a need for excessive admiration, and a lack of empathy for others, individuals with NPD often exhibit specific relationship patterns that can be challenging to navigate. Understanding these patterns is crucial for both those affected by NPD and their loved ones. In this subchapter, we will explore the relationship dynamics commonly observed in individuals with narcissistic personality disorder.

One of the most striking patterns observed in individuals with NPD is their constant need for attention and admiration. They often seek out relationships where they can be the center of attention, expecting others to cater to their every need and desire. This can lead to a power imbalance within relationships, where the narcissistic individual exerts control and manipulates others to maintain their sense of superiority.

Furthermore, individuals with NPD tend to lack genuine empathy and have difficulty understanding and connecting with the emotions of others. This can result in a lack of emotional support and validation within their relationships. They may often invalidate the feelings and experiences of others, dismissing them as insignificant or unworthy of attention. This can leave their partners feeling neglected, unimportant, and emotionally drained.

Another common pattern observed in individuals with NPD is their tendency to exploit and manipulate others for their own gain. They may use charm, flattery, and manipulation tactics to manipulate their partners into meeting their needs and desires. They may also engage in gaslighting, making their partners doubt their own reality and question their sanity.

It is important to note that these relationship patterns are not exclusive to romantic relationships but can also be observed in friendships, familial relationships, and professional settings. Individuals with NPD often struggle with maintaining healthy and balanced relationships across all areas of their lives.

Understanding these relationship patterns is crucial for both individuals with NPD and those in their lives. It can help loved ones set boundaries, establish healthy communication, and protect their own well-being. It can also empower individuals with NPD to seek therapy and work towards developing healthier relationship patterns.

In conclusion, individuals with narcissistic personality disorder often exhibit specific relationship patterns characterized by a constant need for attention and admiration, a lack of empathy, and a tendency to exploit and manipulate others. Recognizing and understanding these patterns is essential for navigating relationships with individuals affected by NPD and promoting healthy connections.

Strategies for dealing with narcissistic individuals

Strategies for dealing with narcissistic individuals:

Narcissistic individuals can be challenging to deal with due to their inflated sense of self-importance, constant need for admiration, and lack of empathy for others. However, understanding effective strategies for interacting with them can help maintain healthier relationships and minimize potential conflicts. In this subchapter, we will explore various strategies for dealing with narcissistic individuals, providing valuable insights for anyone navigating relationships with such individuals.

1. Set Boundaries: Establishing clear boundaries is crucial when dealing with narcissistic individuals. Clearly communicate your needs and expectations, and be firm in enforcing them. Narcissists often push boundaries, so it is important to stand your ground and not allow them to manipulate or take advantage of you.

2. Avoid Engaging in Power Struggles: Narcissistic individuals thrive on power and control. Therefore, it is crucial to avoid engaging in power struggles with them. Instead, focus on maintaining your own emotional well-being and developing healthy coping mechanisms. Refuse to get caught up in their manipulative tactics and stay grounded in your own values and self-worth.

3. Practice Self-Care: Dealing with narcissistic individuals can be emotionally draining. It is essential to prioritize self-care to maintain your own mental and emotional health. Engage in activities that bring you joy, surround yourself with supportive individuals, and seek

professional help if needed. Remember that you deserve to be treated with respect and kindness.

4. Foster Empathy: While narcissistic individuals may struggle with empathy, fostering empathy within yourself can help navigate interactions with them. Try to understand their underlying insecurities and fears, which may manifest as narcissistic behavior. However, it is essential to maintain healthy boundaries and not enable their manipulative actions.

5. Seek Support: Dealing with narcissistic individuals can be a lonely and isolating experience. Reach out to trusted friends, family members, or support groups who can provide guidance, validation, and understanding. Sharing your experiences and learning from others who have faced similar situations can be incredibly empowering.

Remember that dealing with narcissistic individuals requires patience, resilience, and self-reflection. By implementing these strategies, you can protect your own well-being while also fostering healthier relationships with those who may struggle with narcissistic tendencies. Ultimately, the goal is to create a balanced and respectful dynamic that promotes personal growth and connection.

Chapter 6: Borderline Personality Disorder and Relationship Patterns

An overview of borderline personality disorder

Borderline Personality Disorder (BPD) is a complex and often misunderstood mental health condition that affects a significant number of individuals worldwide. This subchapter aims to provide an overview of BPD, shedding light on its definition, symptoms, and potential causes.

BPD is characterized by instability in various aspects of an individual's life, including relationships, emotions, self-image, and behavior. People with BPD often experience intense emotions, which can change rapidly and unpredictably. They may struggle with fear of abandonment, engage in impulsive and self-destructive behaviors, and have difficulty regulating their emotions.

One of the major challenges in diagnosing and understanding BPD lies in its overlapping symptoms with other mental health conditions. However, several criteria are used to identify and diagnose individuals with BPD, including a pattern of unstable relationships, chronic feelings of emptiness, and a distorted sense of self.

The causes of BPD are multifaceted and can be attributed to various factors. While there is no single cause, research suggests that a combination of genetic, environmental, and neurobiological factors may contribute to its development. Childhood trauma, such as physical or sexual abuse, neglect, or the loss of a caregiver, has been identified as a significant risk factor for BPD. Additionally, there may be a genetic predisposition that increases an individual's vulnerability to this disorder.

Understanding the causes of personality disorders, including BPD, is crucial for effective treatment and support. Psychotherapy, particularly Dialectical Behavior Therapy (DBT), has been shown to be highly effective in helping individuals with BPD manage their symptoms and improve their overall well-being. Medication may also be prescribed to address specific symptoms, such as depression or anxiety, that often co-occur with BPD.

It is important to note that individuals with BPD are not defined solely by their diagnosis; they possess unique strengths, experiences, and abilities that contribute to their individuality. Cultivating empathy, compassion, and understanding towards those with BPD is essential to break down the stigma associated with this condition and provide a supportive environment for their recovery.

In conclusion, BPD is a complex personality disorder characterized by emotional instability, difficulties in relationships, and an unstable sense of self. While its causes are multifactorial, a combination of genetic, environmental, and neurobiological factors may contribute to its development. With proper diagnosis and appropriate treatment, individuals with BPD can lead fulfilling lives and establish meaningful connections with others.

Relationship patterns often seen in individuals with borderline personality disorder

Borderline personality disorder (BPD) is a complex mental health condition that affects millions of individuals worldwide. One of the defining characteristics of this disorder is the tumultuous and unstable nature of interpersonal relationships. In this subchapter, we will delve into the relationship patterns often observed in individuals with borderline personality disorder, shedding light on the challenges they face and the impact it has on their lives and those around them.

Individuals with BPD commonly experience intense fear of abandonment, leading to frantic efforts to avoid real or perceived rejection. This fear often manifests in a pattern of clinginess, neediness, and an overwhelming desire for constant reassurance. These individuals may become excessively dependent on their partners, friends, or family members, often expecting them to fulfill all their emotional needs. This intense reliance can strain relationships, as the constant need for validation can be exhausting for the other person involved.

Another common relationship pattern seen in individuals with BPD is a tendency towards extreme idealization and devaluation of others. They may initially idolize and put their partners on a pedestal, believing that they are the perfect solution to their emotional emptiness. However, this idealization is often short-lived, and they quickly shift to devaluing their partners when they inevitably fall short of their unrealistic expectations. This rapid oscillation between extreme admiration and intense disdain can create an unstable and unpredictable environment for those involved in a relationship with someone with BPD.

Furthermore, individuals with BPD often struggle with emotional regulation, which can lead to impulsive behaviors and intense emotional outbursts. This unpredictability can be overwhelming for their partners, friends, and family members, as they may not know how to handle these intense emotions. It can also strain relationships due to impulsive actions such as self-harm, substance abuse, or reckless behaviors.

Understanding these relationship patterns is crucial for individuals with BPD and those around them. It is important to remember that these patterns are not a reflection of their character, but rather a manifestation of their underlying emotional pain and fear of abandonment. By providing empathy, support, and professional help, it is possible to navigate these challenges and foster healthier and more stable relationships.

In conclusion, individuals with borderline personality disorder often exhibit distinct relationship patterns due to their fear of abandonment, idealization and devaluation tendencies, and struggles with emotional regulation. Recognizing and understanding these patterns is essential for both individuals with BPD and their loved ones. With appropriate support and treatment, individuals with BPD can learn healthier ways of relating to others and develop more stable and fulfilling relationships.

The impact of relationship patterns on the symptoms of borderline personality disorder

Borderline personality disorder (BPD) is a complex and often misunderstood mental health condition that affects millions of individuals worldwide. It is characterized by unstable relationships, intense emotions, and a distorted sense of self. While the exact causes of BPD are still being studied, researchers have recognized the significant impact that relationship patterns can have on the symptoms and development of this disorder.

In the book "The Power of Connection: Exploring Relationship Patterns and Personality Development," we delve into the intricate relationship between BPD and the patterns of interpersonal connections. This subchapter aims to shed light on the profound influence that these relationship patterns can have on the causes and symptoms of personality disorders, specifically focusing on BPD.

Research suggests that individuals with BPD often experience difficulties in forming and maintaining stable relationships. Their interactions with others can be characterized by intense emotional reactions, fear of abandonment, and a tendency to idealize or devalue their partners. These relationship patterns play a crucial role in the development and maintenance of BPD symptoms.

Furthermore, growing evidence suggests that adverse childhood experiences, such as neglect, abuse, or inconsistent caregiving, can contribute to the development of BPD. These experiences can shape an individual's attachment style, which influences how they relate to others throughout their lives. For example, those with an anxious attachment style may exhibit clingy or dependent behaviors, whereas individuals with an avoidant attachment style may struggle with emotional intimacy.

Understanding the impact of relationship patterns on BPD symptoms is essential for effective diagnosis and treatment. Therapies that focus on improving interpersonal skills, such as dialectical behavior therapy (DBT), have shown promising results in helping individuals with BPD develop healthier relationship patterns. By addressing the core issues associated with BPD, such as emotional dysregulation and fear of abandonment, these therapies empower individuals to create more stable and fulfilling connections with others.

In conclusion, the relationship patterns that individuals with BPD experience can significantly impact the symptoms and development of the disorder. Recognizing the influence of these patterns is crucial for understanding the causes of personality disorders, including BPD. By exploring the intricate interplay between relationships and mental health, "The Power of Connection" aims to provide valuable insights and support to a wide audience. Whether you are personally affected by BPD or are interested in the causes of personality disorders, this subchapter offers a comprehensive exploration of the impact of relationship patterns on BPD symptoms.

Approaches to managing relationships with individuals with borderline personality disorder

Borderline personality disorder (BPD) is a complex mental health condition that can significantly impact the lives of individuals who experience it, as well as their relationships with others. Managing relationships with someone who has BPD can be challenging, but with the right approaches, it is possible to foster healthier connections and promote a more positive environment for both parties involved.

One crucial aspect of managing relationships with individuals with BPD is understanding the disorder itself. BPD is characterized by intense emotions, unstable self-image, impulsive behavior, and a fear of abandonment. It is important to recognize that these behaviors are not intentional or manipulative but rather a result of the individual's internal struggles. Educating yourself about the causes and symptoms of personality disorders, such as BPD, can help you develop empathy and compassion towards those experiencing it.

One approach to managing relationships with individuals with BPD is maintaining consistent and clear communication. Openly expressing your thoughts and feelings while also actively listening to their concerns can help establish trust and reduce misunderstandings. Additionally, setting and respecting boundaries is crucial. Clearly defining what is acceptable and what is not in the relationship can provide a sense of stability and security for both parties involved.

Another important approach is to encourage therapy and professional support. Individuals with BPD often benefit from therapy, particularly dialectical behavior therapy (DBT), which focuses on developing coping mechanisms and emotional regulation skills. Encouraging your loved one to seek professional help and supporting them throughout their treatment journey can be instrumental in managing their condition and strengthening your relationship.

Self-care is also vital when managing relationships with individuals with BPD. It can be emotionally demanding to support someone with a personality disorder, so it is essential to prioritize your own mental and emotional well-being. Engaging in activities that recharge and rejuvenate you, seeking support from friends or support groups, and setting aside time for self-reflection can help you maintain a healthy balance in your relationships.

In conclusion, managing relationships with individuals with borderline personality disorder requires patience, understanding, and compassion. By educating yourself about the disorder, maintaining open and clear communication, encouraging therapy, and practicing self-care, you can foster healthier connections and create a more positive environment for both yourself and the individual with BPD. Remember, everyone deserves love, understanding, and support, regardless of their mental health condition.

Chapter 7: Antisocial Personality Disorder and Relationship Patterns

Understanding antisocial personality disorder and its relationship patterns

Antisocial personality disorder (ASPD) is a complex mental health condition characterized by a disregard for the rights and feelings of others, coupled with a lack of empathy and remorse. Individuals with this disorder display a consistent pattern of manipulating, exploiting, and violating the rights of others, often leading to significant problems in their personal and social relationships. In this subchapter, we will delve into the intricacies of ASPD and explore its relationship patterns.

One of the key factors in understanding antisocial personality disorder is recognizing the causes behind it. While the exact origins of ASPD are not fully understood, researchers believe that a combination of genetic, environmental, and neurological factors contribute to its development. Childhood trauma, such as physical or emotional abuse, neglect, or inconsistent parenting, is often identified as a risk factor. Additionally, there may be a genetic predisposition that increases the likelihood of developing ASPD.

Understanding the relationship patterns associated with antisocial personality disorder is crucial for both individuals affected by the disorder and those who interact with them. People with ASPD often struggle to form and maintain meaningful relationships due to their disregard for the needs and feelings of others. They may manipulate and exploit others for personal gain, lacking the ability to establish genuine emotional connections. As a result, their relationships are often characterized by a lack of trust, shallow emotional bonds, and a high risk of manipulation and abuse.

It is important to note that not all individuals with antisocial personality disorder exhibit violent or criminal behavior. However, their tendency to exploit and manipulate others can have a significant impact on those around them. Understanding the relationship patterns associated with ASPD can help individuals recognize the signs and protect themselves from potential harm.

In conclusion, understanding antisocial personality disorder and its relationship patterns is crucial for everyone. By recognizing the causes and characteristics of ASPD, we can develop empathy and compassion for individuals with the disorder while also safeguarding ourselves from potential harm. Through education and awareness, we can create a more inclusive and understanding society for individuals affected by antisocial personality disorder and other personality disorders.

The development of antisocial personality disorder

The development of antisocial personality disorder is a complex and multifaceted process that can have profound consequences for individuals and society as a whole. In this subchapter, we will explore the factors that contribute to the emergence of this challenging disorder, shedding light on the causes and potential interventions.

Antisocial personality disorder (ASPD) is characterized by a pervasive pattern of disregard for and violation of the rights of others. People with this disorder often engage in impulsive and irresponsible behaviors, showing little empathy or remorse. Understanding the development of ASPD requires us to examine a range of biological, psychological, and environmental factors.

Biological factors play a crucial role in the development of ASPD. Research suggests that genetic predispositions and abnormalities in brain structure and functioning can contribute to the manifestation of this disorder. For example, certain genetic variations are associated with an increased risk of developing ASPD, while abnormalities in brain regions involved in impulse control and emotional regulation can impair individuals' ability to behave in socially acceptable ways.

Psychological factors also contribute to the development of ASPD. Early childhood experiences, such as neglect, abuse, or inconsistent parenting, can shape a person's personality and increase their vulnerability to developing antisocial tendencies. Additionally, certain personality traits, such as impulsivity, sensation-seeking, and low empathy, can predispose individuals to engage in behaviors that violate social norms.

Environmental factors, including socio-economic disadvantage, exposure to violence, and lack of positive social support, can further exacerbate the development of ASPD. Growing up in a chaotic and unstable environment can hinder the development of prosocial behaviors and reinforce maladaptive coping strategies, increasing the likelihood of developing antisocial traits.

Recognizing the causes of personality disorders, including ASPD, is crucial for effective prevention and intervention strategies. Early identification and intervention can help mitigate the negative impact of risk factors and promote healthier development. Psychotherapy, such as cognitive-behavioral therapy, can help individuals with ASPD develop empathy, impulse control, and more adaptive coping strategies.

In conclusion, the development of antisocial personality disorder is influenced by a complex interplay of biological, psychological, and environmental factors. Understanding these causes can help inform prevention and intervention efforts, ultimately promoting healthier relationship patterns and personality development. By addressing the root causes of personality disorders, we can strive towards a society where everyone has the opportunity to form positive and meaningful connections.

Relationship patterns commonly observed in individuals with antisocial personality disorder

Antisocial personality disorder (ASPD) is a complex mental health condition characterized by a disregard for the rights of others, a lack of empathy, and a pervasive pattern of irresponsible and impulsive behavior. One of the key aspects of ASPD is the impact it has on relationships with others. In this subchapter, we will explore the relationship patterns commonly observed in individuals with antisocial personality disorder.

Individuals with ASPD often struggle with forming and maintaining healthy relationships. They tend to exhibit a range of behaviors that can be highly damaging to those around them. One common pattern is a tendency to manipulate others for personal gain. They may charm and manipulate people to get what they want, without regard for the consequences. This manipulation can be incredibly damaging to those who become entangled in their web of deceit.

Another common relationship pattern in individuals with ASPD is a lack of empathy. They struggle to understand or care about the feelings and needs of others. This can lead to a complete disregard for the well-being of those around them, causing emotional pain and distress. Their lack of empathy often makes it difficult for them to form deep emotional connections, resulting in shallow and superficial relationships.

Individuals with ASPD also tend to engage in impulsive and reckless behaviors, which can strain relationships. They may engage in criminal activities, substance abuse, or engage in risky sexual behavior.

These behaviors not only put their own lives at risk but can also lead to legal issues and strain relationships with family, friends, and partners.

Furthermore, individuals with ASPD often struggle with maintaining long-term commitments. They may engage in serial infidelity or have a history of failed relationships due to their inability to form deep emotional connections. Their erratic behavior and disregard for others' feelings make it challenging for them to sustain healthy and stable relationships.

Understanding these relationship patterns is crucial for anyone interested in the causes of personality disorders. By recognizing the destructive patterns exhibited by individuals with ASPD, we can work towards promoting healthier relationships and providing support for those affected by this condition. It is essential to remember that individuals with ASPD require professional intervention and treatment to address their antisocial behaviors and work towards healthier relationship patterns.

In summary, individuals with antisocial personality disorder often exhibit manipulative behavior, a lack of empathy, engage in impulsive and reckless actions, and struggle to maintain long-term commitments. These relationship patterns can significantly impact the lives of those around them, leading to emotional distress and damage. By understanding these patterns, we can better support individuals with ASPD and work towards healthier relationship dynamics.

Coping strategies for interacting with individuals with antisocial personality disorder

Antisocial personality disorder (ASPD) is a challenging condition that affects both individuals diagnosed with the disorder and those who interact with them. It can be difficult to understand and navigate the complexities of this disorder, but there are coping strategies that can help foster healthier interactions. In this subchapter, we will explore some effective coping strategies for individuals who have loved ones, friends, or colleagues with ASPD.

1. Education and awareness: It is crucial to educate yourself about ASPD, its symptoms, and its impact on relationships. Understanding the disorder can help reduce feelings of confusion, frustration, and blame. By gaining knowledge, you can also develop empathy and compassion towards individuals with ASPD.

2. Setting boundaries: Establishing clear boundaries is essential when interacting with individuals with ASPD. Clearly communicate your expectations and limits in a calm and assertive manner. Consistently enforce these boundaries to establish a sense of stability and predictability.

3. Emotional detachment: People with ASPD may exhibit manipulative behavior or lack empathy. It is important to detach emotionally from their provocative actions and not take them personally. By maintaining emotional distance, you can protect yourself from being manipulated or hurt.

4. Self-care: Taking care of your own mental and emotional well-being is vital when dealing with individuals with ASPD. Engage in activities

that help you relax and recharge. Seek support from friends, family, or support groups to share your experiences and emotions.

5. Communication skills: Developing effective communication skills can help navigate interactions with individuals with ASPD. Use clear, concise language, and avoid emotional outbursts. Stay focused on the facts and avoid becoming entangled in their manipulations or attempts to provoke you.

6. Seek professional help: If you find yourself struggling to cope with the challenges of interacting with individuals with ASPD, consider seeking professional help. Therapists who specialize in personality disorders can provide guidance, support, and coping strategies tailored to your unique situation.

Remember, coping strategies are not a one-size-fits-all solution. It is important to adapt these strategies to your specific circumstances and the nature of the relationship you have with the individual with ASPD. By implementing these coping strategies, you can foster healthier interactions and protect your own well-being while maintaining a connection with individuals who have ASPD.

Chapter 8: Avoidant Personality Disorder and Relationship Patterns

An overview of avoidant personality disorder

In the realm of personality disorders, one particular condition that significantly impacts an individual's ability to form and maintain healthy relationships is known as Avoidant Personality Disorder (AvPD). This subchapter aims to provide an understanding of AvPD, its symptoms, and its impact on personal relationships.

Avoidant Personality Disorder is characterized by persistent feelings of inadequacy, social inhibition, and hypersensitivity to criticism or rejection. Those with AvPD often exhibit an intense fear of rejection and are extremely self-conscious in social situations. As a result, they tend to avoid engaging in activities or forming relationships that might expose them to potential criticism or disapproval.

People with AvPD often experience deep-seated feelings of inferiority and may believe that they are socially inept or unappealing to others. Consequently, they may isolate themselves and develop a preference for solitary activities, leading to a limited social circle or even complete social withdrawal. This isolation exacerbates their feelings of loneliness and reinforces their belief that they are not worthy of companionship.

The causes of AvPD are multifaceted and can be attributed to a combination of genetic, environmental, and psychological factors. Research suggests that individuals with AvPD may have a genetic predisposition towards developing this disorder. Additionally, traumatic experiences, such as childhood neglect or emotional abuse, can contribute to the development of AvPD. These experiences may shape an individual's perception of themselves and others, leading to the adoption of avoidant behaviors as a coping mechanism.

The impact of AvPD on personal relationships is profound. Individuals with AvPD often struggle with forming intimate connections due to their fear of rejection and criticism. They may be hesitant to trust others and may constantly doubt the intentions and loyalty of their partners or friends. This can result in a cycle of failed relationships, reinforcing their belief that they are unlovable and unworthy.

It is important to note that AvPD is a treatable condition, and therapy, particularly cognitive-behavioral therapy, has shown promising results in helping individuals overcome their avoidance behaviors and develop healthier relationship patterns. By addressing the underlying fears and insecurities associated with AvPD, individuals can learn to build meaningful connections and experience more fulfilling relationships.

In conclusion, Avoidant Personality Disorder is a complex condition that significantly affects an individual's ability to form and maintain relationships. Understanding the symptoms, causes, and impact of AvPD is crucial for both individuals struggling with this disorder and those around them. By providing support, education, and access to therapy, we can help individuals with AvPD break free from their avoidance patterns and experience the power of genuine human connection.

Relationship patterns often seen in individuals with avoidant personality disorder

Relationship patterns often seen in individuals with avoidant personality disorder can be complex and challenging to navigate. In this subchapter, we will explore these patterns and shed light on the causes of personality disorders.

Avoidant personality disorder is characterized by a pervasive pattern of social inhibition, feelings of inadequacy, and hypersensitivity to negative evaluation. Those who struggle with this disorder often exhibit specific relationship patterns that can impact their ability to form and maintain connections with others.

One common pattern in individuals with avoidant personality disorder is a fear of rejection and criticism. They may feel unworthy of love and acceptance, leading them to avoid close relationships altogether. This fear can stem from past experiences of rejection or traumatic events that have left a lasting impact on their self-esteem.

Another pattern commonly seen is a tendency to isolate oneself. Individuals with avoidant personality disorder may withdraw from social situations, choosing to spend time alone rather than risk potential rejection or judgment. This isolation can further exacerbate their feelings of loneliness and reinforce their negative self-perceptions.

Additionally, individuals with avoidant personality disorder often struggle with intimacy and trust. They may have a deep longing for connection but struggle to let others in emotionally. This fear of vulnerability can make it difficult for them to form deep, meaningful relationships.

Understanding the causes of personality disorders can provide valuable insight into these relationship patterns. While the exact causes are still being researched, it is believed that a combination of genetic, environmental, and psychological factors contribute to the development of avoidant personality disorder.

Childhood experiences, such as neglect, abuse, or inconsistent parenting, can play a significant role in shaping an individual's personality and their ability to form healthy relationships. Additionally, genetic factors and temperament traits can influence how individuals respond to their environment and cope with stress.

It is essential to approach individuals with avoidant personality disorder with empathy and understanding. Building a supportive and non-judgmental environment can help them feel more comfortable and secure in forming relationships. Therapy, particularly cognitive-behavioral therapy, can be highly effective in helping individuals with avoidant personality disorder develop healthier relationship patterns and improve their overall quality of life.

In conclusion, individuals with avoidant personality disorder often exhibit relationship patterns characterized by fear of rejection, isolation, and difficulty with intimacy and trust. Understanding the causes of personality disorders can shed light on these patterns and guide our approach in supporting individuals with avoidant personality disorder on their journey towards healthier relationships.

The impact of relationship patterns on the symptoms of avoidant personality disorder

In the fascinating world of human psychology, the causes of personality disorders have long been a subject of great interest and debate. Different theories suggest that a combination of genetic factors, childhood experiences, and environmental influences contribute to the development of these disturbances in personality. One such disorder that has gained significant attention is avoidant personality disorder (APD).

In our book, "The Power of Connection: Exploring Relationship Patterns and Personality Development," we delve into the impact of relationship patterns on the symptoms of APD. This subchapter aims to shed light on the complex interplay between relationships and the manifestation of this disorder, with the ultimate goal of fostering understanding and empathy for individuals who struggle with APD.

Avoidant personality disorder is characterized by an overwhelming fear of rejection, leading those affected to avoid social interactions and intimacy. While genetic and biological factors play a role, the relationship patterns individuals develop in their formative years can significantly exacerbate or alleviate the symptoms of APD.

Children who grow up in households where they are consistently criticized, neglected, or rejected are more likely to develop avoidant traits as a coping mechanism. These negative relationship patterns teach individuals to anticipate rejection and view others as potential threats. Consequently, they withdraw from social situations, depriving themselves of the connections they desperately crave.

Furthermore, studies have shown that individuals with APD often struggle with attachment issues. They may have experienced inconsistent or insecure attachments during their early years, leading them to develop an avoidant attachment style characterized by emotional distance and detachment from others. This attachment style perpetuates a vicious cycle, as it reinforces their fears of rejection and perpetuates their avoidance of close relationships.

Understanding the impact of relationship patterns on the symptoms of APD is crucial for effective treatment and support. Therapeutic interventions that focus on building trust, fostering secure attachments, and challenging negative cognitive patterns can help individuals with APD overcome their fear and develop healthier relationship patterns.

In conclusion, the relationship patterns individuals develop, particularly in their formative years, can significantly impact the symptoms of avoidant personality disorder. By exploring these patterns and their effects, we hope to promote empathy, understanding, and effective interventions for individuals struggling with APD. Through connection and support, we can help individuals break free from the chains of fear and isolation, enabling them to embrace fulfilling relationships and lead more satisfying lives.

Approaches to building healthy relationships with individuals with avoidant personality disorder

Introduction:

In this subchapter, we will explore effective approaches to building healthy relationships with individuals who have Avoidant Personality Disorder (AVPD). Understanding the causes of personality disorders is crucial to developing empathy and adopting appropriate strategies. By recognizing the challenges faced by those with AVPD, we can foster meaningful connections and help them overcome their difficulties in interpersonal relationships.

1. Educating Yourself:
To establish healthy relationships with individuals with AVPD, it is essential to familiarize yourself with the disorder's characteristics and symptoms. Understanding that their avoidance stems from feelings of inadequacy and fear of rejection can help you approach them with empathy and patience.

2. Creating a Safe and Non-Threatening Environment:
Individuals with AVPD often feel anxious and uncomfortable in social situations. To build a healthy relationship, it is crucial to create a safe, non-threatening environment. Avoid pressuring or criticizing them, as this may reinforce their avoidance. Instead, provide reassurance and understanding, allowing them to express themselves at their own pace.

3. Encouraging Open Communication:
Effective communication is vital when building relationships with individuals with AVPD. Encourage them to express their thoughts and emotions, even if they may seem hesitant or reserved. Active listening

and validating their feelings are key to establishing trust and demonstrating that you genuinely care about their well-being.

4. Setting Realistic Expectations:
Individuals with AVPD often struggle with intimacy and may find it challenging to maintain close relationships. It is important to set realistic expectations and respect their boundaries. Pushing for more than they are comfortable with may trigger their avoidance behaviors. Patience and understanding are crucial in slowly building trust over time.

5. Offering Support and Encouragement:
Individuals with AVPD often have low self-esteem and doubt their abilities to form meaningful connections. Offering support and encouragement can help boost their confidence and foster a healthier self-image. Celebrate their achievements, no matter how small, and provide constructive feedback to help them grow.

Conclusion:
Building healthy relationships with individuals with Avoidant Personality Disorder requires empathy, understanding, and patience. By educating ourselves about the causes and symptoms of AVPD, creating a safe environment, encouraging open communication, setting realistic expectations, and offering support, we can help individuals with AVPD develop more fulfilling and meaningful connections. Remember, every individual deserves love, understanding, and a chance to thrive in healthy relationships.

Chapter 9: Healing and Transforming Relationship Patterns

Recognizing and acknowledging unhealthy relationship patterns

In the journey of exploring relationship patterns and personality development, it is crucial to acknowledge and recognize unhealthy relationship patterns. These patterns can have a profound impact on our lives and the lives of those around us. Understanding the causes of personality disorders can provide valuable insights into why these patterns develop and how they can be addressed.

Unhealthy relationship patterns can manifest in various ways, including codependency, manipulation, emotional abuse, and control. It is essential to recognize these patterns because they can lead to detrimental consequences for our mental and emotional well-being. By acknowledging them, we can take the necessary steps to break free from these destructive cycles.

One of the causes of personality disorders is often rooted in childhood experiences. Trauma, neglect, or inconsistent parenting can shape our beliefs and behaviors, leading to unhealthy relationship patterns later in life. Recognizing these underlying factors can help us understand why we may be prone to certain patterns and allow us to address them effectively.

Another cause of personality disorders can be attributed to societal influences and cultural norms. For example, toxic masculinity, which places an emphasis on dominance and control, can contribute to the development of unhealthy relationship patterns. Recognizing these external influences can empower us to challenge and change these destructive patterns.

Recognizing unhealthy relationship patterns requires self-reflection and self-awareness. It involves examining our thoughts, emotions, and actions within the context of our relationships. This introspection allows us to identify patterns that may be detrimental to our own well-being or the well-being of those around us.

Acknowledging these patterns is the first step towards breaking free from them. It requires courage and a willingness to confront uncomfortable truths about ourselves and our relationships. However, by doing so, we gain the power to make positive changes and cultivate healthy connections.

In conclusion, recognizing and acknowledging unhealthy relationship patterns is essential for personal growth and development. By understanding the causes of personality disorders and the societal influences that contribute to them, we can gain a deeper understanding of ourselves and our relationships. This knowledge empowers us to break free from destructive cycles and create healthier, more fulfilling connections. Remember, it is never too late to recognize and address these patterns – the power to change lies within each and every one of us.

Strategies for breaking free from dysfunctional relationship patterns

In the journey of personal growth and development, it is crucial to recognize and address dysfunctional relationship patterns that may be holding us back. Whether it is a romantic relationship, friendship, or even familial ties, breaking free from these patterns can be a transformative experience. This subchapter aims to provide strategies for individuals seeking to escape dysfunctional relationship patterns and create healthier connections in their lives.

1. Self-reflection and awareness: The first step towards breaking free from dysfunctional relationship patterns is to reflect on oneself and become aware of the underlying causes and triggers. Understanding the root causes of these patterns, such as childhood experiences or past traumas, can help individuals gain clarity and make informed choices moving forward.

2. Seek professional help: Seeking therapy or counseling from a trained professional can be immensely valuable in exploring and overcoming dysfunctional relationship patterns. A mental health professional can provide guidance, support, and tools to navigate the complexities of these patterns, allowing individuals to develop healthier relationship habits.

3. Set boundaries: Establishing healthy boundaries is essential in breaking free from dysfunctional relationship patterns. Clearly defining what is acceptable and what is not in relationships can prevent toxic dynamics from reoccurring. Learning to say no and prioritizing self-care are crucial steps in setting and maintaining boundaries.

4. Surround yourself with positive influences: Surrounding oneself with positive and supportive people can significantly impact one's ability to break free from dysfunctional relationship patterns. Seek out individuals who uplift and inspire you, as they can serve as role models for healthy relationships.

5. Practice self-love and self-care: Cultivating self-love and prioritizing self-care are essential strategies for breaking free from dysfunctional relationship patterns. Engage in activities that bring you joy, practice self-compassion, and focus on personal growth. This will not only boost your self-esteem but also attract healthier relationships into your life.

6. Learn from past experiences: Reflect on past relationships and identify recurring patterns or red flags. Learning from these experiences can help you avoid making the same mistakes and make more informed choices in future relationships.

Breaking free from dysfunctional relationship patterns is a process that requires patience, self-reflection, and conscious effort. By implementing these strategies, individuals can empower themselves to create healthier relationships and promote personal growth. Remember, it is never too late to break free and build the connections we truly deserve.

Building healthy relationship patterns for personal growth and development

Building healthy relationship patterns is essential for personal growth and development. In order to understand the importance of cultivating healthy relationships, it is crucial to explore the causes of personality disorders. By addressing these causes, we can gain insight into how to build healthier relationships and foster personal growth.

Personality disorders stem from various factors, including genetic predispositions, childhood experiences, and environmental influences. Understanding the causes helps us recognize the patterns that lead to unhealthy relationships and ultimately hinder our personal development. By identifying these patterns, we can work towards breaking free from negative cycles and creating positive change.

One significant cause of personality disorders is childhood trauma or adverse experiences. Negative experiences during childhood, such as abuse, neglect, or inconsistent parenting, can shape our beliefs and behaviors in relationships. These early experiences can lead to unhealthy attachment styles, fear of intimacy, or difficulties in trust and communication. By acknowledging the impact of childhood trauma, we can begin to heal and develop healthier relationship patterns.

Another cause of personality disorders is a lack of healthy role models. Growing up in an environment where there is a lack of positive relationship models can hinder our ability to form healthy connections. It is important to seek out positive role models, mentors, or therapists who can provide guidance and support in building healthy relationship patterns.

Environmental factors, such as societal expectations or cultural norms, can also contribute to the development of personality disorders. Societal pressures to conform or meet certain standards can lead to feelings of inadequacy or low self-worth. Recognizing and challenging these external influences can help us develop a more authentic and healthy sense of self, leading to healthier relationships.

To build healthy relationship patterns, it is essential to prioritize self-care and self-awareness. Taking care of our physical, emotional, and mental well-being allows us to show up as our best selves in relationships. Self-awareness involves recognizing our own patterns, triggers, and limitations. This self-reflection enables us to communicate effectively, set boundaries, and cultivate empathy towards ourselves and others.

In conclusion, building healthy relationship patterns is crucial for personal growth and development. Exploring the causes of personality disorders helps us understand the patterns that hinder our progress. By addressing these causes and focusing on self-care and self-awareness, we can break free from negative cycles and foster healthier relationships. Building healthy relationships is a lifelong journey, but one that is essential for our well-being and personal growth.

Seeking professional help for healing and transforming relationship patterns

In our journey through life, our relationships play a vital role in shaping our personality and overall well-being. However, sometimes we find ourselves trapped in negative relationship patterns that hinder our growth and happiness. Whether it's constantly finding ourselves in toxic relationships, struggling to maintain healthy boundaries, or repeating the same destructive behaviors, seeking professional help can be an empowering step towards healing and transforming these patterns.

Understanding the causes of personality disorders is crucial in our quest for personal growth. Personality disorders can arise from a variety of factors, such as genetics, childhood experiences, trauma, or a combination of these. These disorders can significantly impact our ability to form and maintain healthy relationships, affecting our emotional and psychological well-being. Recognizing the underlying causes of these patterns is the first step towards seeking professional help.

Professional help provides a safe and supportive environment where individuals can explore their relationship patterns and gain valuable insights into their behavior. Through therapy, counseling, or support groups, individuals can learn to identify and challenge negative patterns, develop healthy coping mechanisms, and improve their overall emotional intelligence. Skilled professionals can guide individuals through the process of self-discovery, helping them uncover the root causes of their relationship patterns and providing them with the tools to break free from destructive cycles.

Seeking professional help does not signify weakness; rather, it showcases strength and the desire for personal growth. It takes courage to acknowledge that we need assistance in navigating our relationships and transforming negative patterns. Professional help provides a non-judgmental space where individuals can openly express their emotions, fears, and desires, and receive guidance in a compassionate and understanding manner.

Moreover, seeking professional help not only benefits the individual but also the people around them. By addressing and resolving our relationship patterns, we create healthier and more fulfilling connections with our loved ones, friends, and colleagues. Our transformed patterns can positively impact all aspects of our lives, leading to greater personal satisfaction, improved mental health, and enhanced overall well-being.

In conclusion, seeking professional help for healing and transforming relationship patterns is a crucial step towards personal growth and happiness. Regardless of the causes of personality disorders, professional support provides individuals with the necessary tools to identify, challenge, and transform negative patterns. It is an empowering process that allows individuals to break free from destructive cycles and develop healthier, more fulfilling relationships. By seeking professional help, we take control of our lives and pave the way for a brighter future filled with meaningful connections and personal transformation.

Chapter 10: Conclusion

Recap of key points discussed in the book

"The Power of Connection: Exploring Relationship Patterns and Personality Development"

Personality disorders have long been a subject of interest and concern in the field of psychology. In our book, "The Power of Connection: Exploring Relationship Patterns and Personality Development," we have delved into the causes of personality disorders and shed light on the importance of understanding relationship patterns for personal growth and development.

Throughout the book, we have emphasized the significance of early childhood experiences in shaping one's personality. These experiences, particularly those involving significant relationships with caregivers, can have a profound impact on how individuals perceive themselves and interact with others. Negative or traumatic experiences during this critical period can contribute to the development of personality disorders later in life.

We have also discussed the role of genetics and biology in the manifestation of personality disorders. While environmental factors play a significant role, there is evidence to suggest a genetic predisposition to certain personality traits and disorders. Understanding this interplay between nature and nurture is crucial for comprehending the causes of personality disorders fully.

Furthermore, we have examined the influence of social and cultural factors on personality development. Society's expectations, cultural norms, and social pressures can shape individuals' personalities and contribute to the development of maladaptive patterns of behavior. Recognizing these external influences is essential for understanding the causes of personality disorders and implementing effective interventions.

In addition to exploring the causes of personality disorders, we have highlighted the importance of building healthy relationships. We have emphasized the power of connection and its potential to positively influence personality development. By fostering secure attachments, practicing effective communication, and developing emotional intelligence, individuals can enhance their overall well-being and mitigate the risk of developing personality disorders.

Throughout the book, we have aimed to provide a comprehensive overview of the causes of personality disorders while offering practical insights into building healthier relationships. By understanding the interplay of genetics, early experiences, social factors, and personal choices, individuals can gain valuable insights into their own personality development and work towards personal growth and fulfillment.

"The Power of Connection: Exploring Relationship Patterns and Personality Development" is a valuable resource for anyone interested in understanding the causes of personality disorders and discovering strategies for building healthier relationships. Whether you are a mental health professional, a student, or an individual seeking personal growth, this book provides a comprehensive exploration of these topics and empowers you to take control of your own development.

The importance of self-awareness and self-reflection in relationship patterns

In our journey through life, we are constantly forming connections with others. These relationships play a significant role in shaping our personality and overall development. However, have you ever stopped and wondered why certain relationship patterns seem to repeat themselves? Why do we find ourselves attracted to the same type of people or experiencing similar conflicts in our relationships?

The answer lies in self-awareness and self-reflection. These two powerful tools are essential for understanding our relationship patterns and uncovering the causes of personality disorders. By exploring our own thoughts, emotions, and behaviors, we can gain valuable insights into why we engage in certain relationship dynamics.

Self-awareness is the ability to recognize and understand our own thoughts, emotions, and actions. It allows us to become conscious of our patterns, preferences, and triggers in relationships. By being self-aware, we can identify recurring themes in our interactions and acknowledge any destructive patterns that may be present. For example, if we find ourselves constantly seeking validation from others, we can start to understand the underlying insecurities that drive this behavior.

Self-reflection, on the other hand, involves deep introspection and examination of our own experiences and actions. It allows us to dive beneath the surface and explore the root causes of our relationship patterns. Through self-reflection, we can identify unresolved traumas, childhood experiences, or negative beliefs that may be influencing how we engage with others. By understanding these underlying factors, we can begin to heal and break free from destructive relationship patterns.

The importance of self-awareness and self-reflection in relationship patterns cannot be overstated. Without these tools, we are doomed to repeat the same mistakes and fall into unfulfilling or toxic relationships. By developing self-awareness and engaging in self-reflection, we can gain a deeper understanding of ourselves and our needs. This understanding allows us to make conscious choices in our relationships, attract healthier partners, and create more fulfilling connections.

For those struggling with personality disorders, self-awareness and self-reflection are even more crucial. These disorders often stem from deep-seated issues, and exploring our relationship patterns can offer invaluable insights into their causes. By delving into our past and examining our present behaviors, we can start to untangle the complex web of factors contributing to our personality disorders.

In conclusion, self-awareness and self-reflection are essential tools for understanding our relationship patterns and uncovering the causes of personality disorders. By developing these skills, we can break free from destructive patterns, attract healthier relationships, and embark on a journey of self-discovery and personal growth. So, take the time to explore yourself, your thoughts, and your actions. The power to transform your relationships and enhance your well-being lies within your own self-awareness and self-reflection.

Embracing healthy relationship patterns for personal and interpersonal growth

In the journey of personal and interpersonal growth, one of the most crucial aspects is the development of healthy relationship patterns. Relationships play a significant role in shaping our personality and overall well-being. Whether it's with our family, friends, or romantic partners, the quality of our relationships directly impacts our emotional, mental, and even physical health. In this subchapter, we will explore why embracing healthy relationship patterns is essential for personal growth and how it can contribute to the prevention and understanding of personality disorders.

Firstly, it is important to understand the causes of personality disorders. These disorders often arise from a combination of genetic, biological, and environmental factors. However, one cannot overlook the impact of unhealthy relationship patterns on the development of such disorders. Traumatic experiences, neglect, abuse, or inconsistent parenting can significantly influence the formation of maladaptive patterns in individuals, leading to personality disorders later in life. Therefore, by understanding the role of relationships in the development of personality disorders, we can strive to prevent and avoid perpetuating these harmful patterns.

Embracing healthy relationship patterns is a fundamental step towards personal growth. Healthy relationships are built on mutual respect, trust, effective communication, and emotional support. By cultivating these qualities in our relationships, we create a nurturing and positive environment for personal development. Healthy relationships provide a sense of belonging, security, and acceptance, allowing individuals to explore their true potential and flourish in various aspects of life. When we surround ourselves with healthy relationships, we are more likely to experience higher self-esteem, improved mental health, and enhanced overall well-being.

Moreover, healthy relationship patterns also contribute to interpersonal growth. By embodying healthy communication and conflict resolution skills, we can build stronger and more fulfilling connections with others. Understanding the needs and boundaries of both ourselves and others in a relationship fosters empathy, compassion, and understanding. This, in turn, promotes harmonious interactions, reduces conflicts, and leads to deeper and more meaningful connections with those around us.

In conclusion, embracing healthy relationship patterns is crucial for personal and interpersonal growth. By understanding the causes of personality disorders, we can identify the role of unhealthy relationships in their development. By cultivating healthy relationships based on respect, trust, and effective communication, we create an environment that fosters personal growth and prevents the perpetuation of harmful patterns. Embracing healthy relationship patterns not only benefits individuals but also contributes to the overall well-being of society as a whole. Let us strive to build and nurture healthy relationships for our own personal growth and the betterment of our relationships and communities.

Final thoughts on the power of connection and its impact on personality development

In this subchapter, we will delve deeper into the profound influence of connection on personality development and its role in shaping our lives. Understanding the power of connection is crucial, as it can lead to a deeper comprehension of the causes of personality disorders. By exploring the intricate relationship patterns that emerge from our connections, we can gain valuable insights into the development of these disorders.

Connection is a fundamental aspect of human existence. From the moment we are born, we seek connection with others. It is through connection that we form our identities and develop a sense of self. Our relationships, whether they are healthy or dysfunctional, significantly impact our personality development.

The causes of personality disorders are complex and multifaceted. However, one common thread that emerges is the lack of healthy and secure connections during critical stages of development. When individuals experience consistent rejection, neglect, or abuse, their personality development can be greatly affected. These negative experiences can hinder their ability to form healthy relationships and can lead to the manifestation of personality disorders.

On the other hand, positive and nurturing connections can foster healthy personality development. When individuals experience love, support, and empathy, they are more likely to develop a strong sense of self and healthy relationship patterns. These connections provide a foundation for emotional resilience and the ability to navigate challenges in life.

It is crucial for EVERY ONE to recognize the power of connection and its impact on personality development. By understanding the causes of personality disorders, we can make a difference in the lives of those affected. We can work towards creating supportive environments that prioritize healthy connections and provide individuals with the tools they need to develop their personalities in a positive way.

Moreover, EACH ONE of us can play a role in promoting healthy connections. By fostering empathy, compassion, and understanding, we can contribute to the creation of a society that values healthy relationships. We can educate ourselves and others about the importance of connection, and work towards breaking the cycle of negative relationship patterns.

In conclusion, the power of connection cannot be underestimated when it comes to personality development and the causes of personality disorders. It is through our connections that we shape our identities and develop a sense of self. By recognizing the impact of connection and working towards fostering healthy relationships, we can make a positive difference in the lives of individuals affected by personality disorders. Let us embrace the power of connection and strive towards creating a world where everyone can experience the transformative effects of healthy connections.

www.ingramcontent.com/pod-product-compliance
Lightning Source LLC
LaVergne TN
LVHW051958060526
838201LV00059B/3707